a clear day in october

D1516105

j. lewis

poetry & photography

edited by Brian James Lewis

a clear day in october

10 9 8 7 6 5 4 3 2 1

ISBN: 978-1-68073-055-5 (Trade Paperback)
ISBN: 978-1-68073-056-2 (Kindle)

Empire & Great Jones Little Press is wholly operated by the Empire & Great Jones
Creative Arts Foundation, a registered 501(c)(3) non-profit corporation.

Empire & Great Jones Creative Arts Foundation
Brian Lewis, President
6100 Horseshoe Bar Road, Suite A-133
Loomis, CA 95650
USA

about the poet

Jim Lewis is an internationally-published poet described by his friends as a Renaissance Man, multi-talented, remarkable, or sometimes as "odd, but in a good way." By profession, he is a certified Family Nurse Practitioner, with a parallel career in technology. By hobby, he is a musician, writer, photographer, and kayaker.

Jim's interest in writing goes back to his early youth, but he only started to send out his poetry to editors and publishers when he reached his sixties. To his surprise and delight, several pieces were quickly accepted for publication, and so for the first time he envisioned a collection of his favorite poems.

These hand-picked favorites have been paired with his own photography to share with you as *a clear day in october*.

about the editor

Brian James Lewis is an active member of the Editorial Freelancers Association, an alumnus of the California State Summer School for the Arts in Creative Writing, and a software security architect. He is president of the Empire & Great Jones Creative Arts Foundation. Brian and his wife live in the town of Loomis, California, with their eight children—who all love reading.

Brian James Lewis is also Jim's oldest son.

contents

foreword

Forward!

I was stunned and honored when j.lewis invited me to write the foreword for his first full-length collection of poetry, so much so that I agreed without thinking ahead about how exactly I would manage to do that.

My expectation of a foreword is that it serves as an introduction, something along the lines of "Reader, meet Poet." But how do I go about introducing a poet who has written the line "*i never felt i needed describing*"?

Alternatively, a foreword can serve as history and prescription, explain where the poems came from, and what the reader ought to think of them. But I can't pretend to know either of those things well enough to blithely presume to tell you. Or you. Or you.

So how do I set your expectations so that you are somehow prepared before you begin to turn the pages? Offer up a pre-departure checklist? Bring your eyes, there are exquisite pictures. Bring your appetite, there's pizza. Bring your ears, there's music so loud you can hear it.

Dust off your own memories of childhood desires and disappointments. Open the quiet closet of your experiences as a parent. Find the twins—reverence and irreverence—bring them both. Bring along the bridges you have crossed, bring the ashes of the ones that you have burned.

Clean the surface of whatever device on which you receive the news of grief in other places, other cultures, other nations. You are cleared through security to travel, enter hospitals and prisons. Tuck a handkerchief discretely in your pocket just in case.

Are you ready to walk past empty rooms, sit in a café, read a recipe for sacrifice and faith? Are you ready for rain, for grief? Are you willing to slop pigs? Are you willing to be torn and mended, blessed?

Then come, and welcome. You're invited to make your own contrails across this sky, across this clear day in October.

Forward!

Laura M Kaminski

salieri's lament

heaven plays its humor out in men like me
plants in us desire to sing praises
the full fruit of our talent, sweet—
but common and pale
beside the flower of genius

such an ungodly prank
to fill me with yearning
then give another the voice of my songs
music i have dreamed and forgotten at waking
lines and phrases of eternal echoes
revealed in details i can't write
that dissolve to simple melodies
and little pleasantries
for the popular court

what loving creator would place me here
driven to produce, then reduced
to grudging applause of the upstart genius
who thanks me for a trifle composed in his honor
then having played it once
criticizes and improves impromptu
infuriatingly right
with every remake and remark
making me less a heavenly handiwork
more a celestial satire

who will remember i was here
when no one notices the shadows
that make the light more bright?

surgical mass

quiet hovers in this sacred place
the last vestiges of uncleanliness
scoured away this morning
before dawn

a priestess enters unspeaking
spreads the utensils of the first
    sacrament
with practiced ease
across the twice blessed stand
saving for last
three basins of consecrated water

a second priestess enters, nods
and sets about preparing the altar
draping it in layers of holy cloth
reverent attention to every folded
    corner

a heavy door groans open
as cardinal and claustral converge
hands raised in traditional defer-
    ence
to those who sanctified them
for this work

in a flurry of activity
they are robed head to toe
in heavenly blue
every element of the common
    world
covered against the chance
that some small sin
may yet cling to them
and falling unchecked
defile the offering

the sacramental emblem arrives
prepared and positioned
precisely

with an upward glance
at the clock high on the wall
the priest grips his blade
brow wrinkled in concentration
"nine o'clock" he incants
"midline incision
xyphoid to umbilicus"

empty

the hallway is quiet tonight
like last night and the one before
yet i hear his voice from the room
where he daily tried to hide
from loneliness and depression
moving in and out of
sleep and music
sleep and books
sleep and more sleep
sliding down, ever down
until i couldn't reach him anymore

we ground against each other
sheets of coarse sandpaper
determined not to lose
destined not to win

somewhere along the way, love got lost
and liking him was buried
in the bits and pieces
we tore from each other
i could not find forgiveness
only resignation and commitment

my conscience burns at this sense of relief
ashamed that the silence is pleasant

i walk the hallway past his room
his absence shouts pain, anger
and sadness too deep to measure
an awkward loneliness surprises me
as I realize that this room
will never be truly
empty

empty refilled

the hallway would be quiet again tonight
like all the nights this week
except i hear his voice
from the quasi-empty room
where he is but isn't quite
though we brought him home today

it is eerie
watching someone you should know
skating in a parallel universe
reflecting reality imperfectly
convinced in black and white certainty
that his world is the only truth
and so irritable that
a single syllable angers him

he wants to be waited on
bitterly complains of boredom so broad
that sleep—the endless variety
would be better

we cannot entertain him
he will not move to entertain himself
his logic runs in circles, counters our suggestions
arguing with conviction that nothing will interest him
refusing to try, looking instead
to interrupt his ennui with confrontation
contention and anger
i will not play
that game again with him

the roller-coaster drains me
last night it was sadness
guilt at the empty room

tonight is frustration
and fear of this familiar stranger
who dictates my life
from his dream-world throne
until i find I am eager again
to have him go
knowing he is already gone

under the bridge

navajo, my parents said
we will live on the reservation
but eight years old was not enough
to measure the importance of the move

i didn't know it should have made
my father's life less hell
only that my daydreams
and my treasure box
went north out of familiar walls
green grass and the crab apple tree
to sage brush, sand, and wind

nine is not enough to know
words like depression and despair
but i lived them there
the trading post and house
surrounded by miles of nothing

the bridge was just a bridge on top
but underneath
the wooden beams, dark with creosote
had offered some unschooled talent
a canvas for his fantasies
his brush a piece of chalk

ten was not enough to know
of coupling and such
and the revelation of differences
frightened and intrigued me
the short walk to the bridge
became a daily pilgrimage
to see if some new knowledge
had been inscribed

white lines of passion
on greasy brown boards

when the flash floods came
they washed away
the illicit illustrations
left me with no reason to return
except the packed sand banks
where i went back to being eleven
and carved out a city
for my matchbox cars

Before I Go

Every line must end correctly here,
Every verb be in a perfect tense.
It's been so long since I last read your voice
And if I had my way, my simple choice
Would be to trim the distance (too immense)
Between us, make you miles and miles more near.
And then, come autumn wind or winter snow,
I'd see you wave and smile, before I go.

asthma

the wind rattles everything it passes
in its long trek through these canyons
flowing cool and dry before sunrise
shaking scrub juniper that keeps a death grip
on crimson sandstone walls
rippling the muddy stream that snakes
randomly down eroded trails

wheezing back in evening's dimming light
hot and moist and angry at every twist
every turn and obstruction that stands
between it and canyon's gaping mouth
where it escapes, dying into a fitful breeze
that barely rustles the gray sage
eddying restlessly, impatient
for the dawn's quiet summons
to race the stiffened channels once again

fibrillation

impulse on impulse
tiny sparks of life
unregulated
chaotic
electrical nomads
wandering the atrial desert
ignorant of the harm they do
in their
  aimless
    endless
      journey

cardioversion

quietly
carefully
forces marshal,
spies strategically scattered,
enemy surrounded—
every move monitored

then
the blitzkrieg arcs
stuns
and disappears
leaving a lone survivor
to tap out
his singular signal

lake fog

i felt it in my sleep
lake fog laying siege
to near-defenseless thoughts

no dainty creeping in
on little cat-feet
the voracious mist
reeked of dead fish
and lost dreams
accused me of wasted days
forgotten loves
life half-lived
and hidden sorrows

lemmings

think not on lemmings lest you follow on
and following fall upon the sea
which wants not lemming-flavored waves
but opens to eat them anyway

unstrung

when the day ends
pulls a shade down
on the sun of all you are
i will play your song
and then
put my guitar to rest
each silver string released
tucked away
in coils of remembering
and i will wait
find ways to pass the time
without the music
of you with me
when the day comes
that you leave me
all unstrung

and if i dream

some fear
and some desire
shakespeare's undiscovered country
reluctant or eager in turn
to know its secrets
halting or hasting
to dreams they have not dreamed

i feel no fear, no attraction
see only that someday
i must travel there
where all mankind makes pilgrimage

what comes will come
and if i dream
my dreams will all be color
bold and bright
brush and oils borrowed
from years of you and me
sorrow and ecstasy
small moments and quiet glances
across a room, across eternity
the canvas is unchanged
what our lives have arranged
death cannot alter

breakup

so then there were tears again
salt and acid bitter drops
that burned irregular roads
asymmetrical highways
down the map of her face

she looked at me finally
sorry eyes and full of red
that could have meant anything
or nothing kept inside her
perhaps an unformed question

i had an answer ready
she should have let me play it
a carefully metered thing
to counteract her leaving

i couldn't even exhale

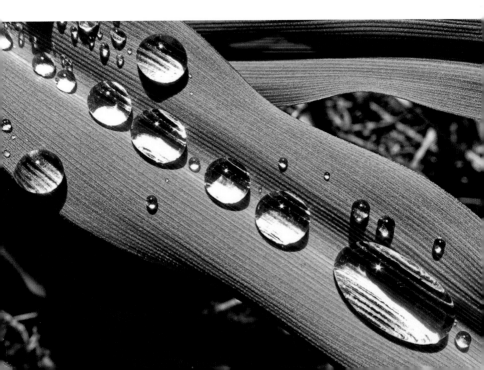

endless

there is a rhythm
to the halting, jerking motion
of a farmer's cart
across furrowed fields
an eternity of corn stalks
dry and bundled for harvest
a reaping among the ruts
that go on without change
planting a day and night cycle
metered by the relentless
thump
bump
scrape
of farmer's back
on wooden cart-seat

sky, field, trees and earth
cast a make-shift frame
around the trio
of man, cart, and horse
and only the horse knows
they aren't going anywhere

andrew in the evening

her place:
evening is hard he said
moving between this world and the other
guarding my words
tending with such care
the fences i have built
to make this little place in my life
i weary of the deception
but no solutions come
conscience urges me to give you up
pull the curtain, cover the inspiration you are
and paint my kitchen window
or the pastor's children
but then something of me would die—

he paused and noticed
she was quietly arranging her hair and her collar
smiling at the familiar monologue
knowing he would return
that she would give him what she could give
no fear and no regret
paint what your heart sees
she said simply
i will be here

his place:
evening is hard he said
stopping to kiss her hello
and sample the stew that simmered
like his passion for things beautiful
i am driven to create
and some days it just doesn't work
the colors are wrong
the light in the waves mocks me and eludes me
maybe i should paint the kitchen window
or the pastor's children—

he paused and noticed
she was quietly arranging the plates at table
knowing he would never quit until he got it right
she would continue to give him all she could give
no recrimination, no looking back
paint what your heart sees
she said simply
i will be here

red bridge

there was a vague point
at which he stopped counting
the hours, days, weeks
since rejection
nothing specific to hail
and say hooray, hoorah
she doesn't matter enough
to keep this calendar vigil

all that ties him to her
is a vivid photograph
of a red bridge
where they fed giant koi
and marveled at how huge
each fish had grown

and in perfect
unintended symbolism
the bridge
that blood-red bridge
is absolutely empty

All I Want

Wife in the grave for sixteen years,
son in the pen for life,
and all I want
is to outlive my dog
because no one else will love her
like I do.

castle and tide

ebb and timeless flow
protection and threat
water, moving water
surrounds and separates
rises to kiss foundation stone
falls away revealing
bareness, dark soil, hard rock

and so you are
as the tides around me
constant motion
deep devotion played against
my gray unyielding walls
you never fail
i never fall

avalanche

the buildup was unmonitored
in the frequency of storms
an occasional thought of caution
lost in adversarial winds
that whipped across each day
hard, cold, biting

today under an almost sunny sky
a single word dropped like an acorn
in the days and weeks of snow

an infinity of small events
holding desperately together
lost their communal grip
roared down rocky terrain, buried everything
and everyone below in cold fury
leaving at the mountain's top
unexpected emptiness, bareness
depression

fear

fear like a fire
flickers
then flares
burns me inside out
an endless flame

fear like solid ice
forms deep within
shivers me
freezes over my heart
chills my mind

fear omnivorous
eats away my lining
hungry, whining
everything is gone

early winter

there is something in the air
a feel of autumn
hinting of frost
and separation
from the easy sun of summer
chilly prophecies
of wintry death
of ground once soft and fertile
frozen too deep
for plow to penetrate

i savor the years when
the promise of spring
kept the freezing wind at bay
walling me in warm anticipation

spring fields
for Emily

the perennial plowing
turning of the soil
are meanings and methods
lost on ground that lies
free of imagination,
the pressure of the sower's foot
an insult above the injury inflicted

in the cycle of sun and water
hot days and cold nights
sprouting seeds (innocent, ambitious)
hold carefully to the scars of turned earth
find in its disruption the food of life

through the seductive summer
plants, sweet and green
ripen to golden bounty
proud and beautiful
only to fall beneath the hand
of the harvester

winter wraps the stubble
in a merciful blanket
hides from critical eyes
the grief and slow healing
the renewing that must come
before the new year
and the sudden piercing plow

i know the puzzled pain
of a heart harrowed in spring
by new love's preparation—
know too the euphoric
heavy-scented nights
of love in full bloom
and the agony
of love gone too soon
in the california haze
harvest over

i watch the snow
drift over this most recent reaping
and hope you winter well

goodbye sounds like

when you are the passenger
no dash-mount panic handle
car and driver
taking the corner hard
hearing tires complain
in their own peculiar voice
shouting goodbye to pavement
soon to be abandoned

stomach tightens
and a frightened breath in
betrays you to the one
who grips your heart hard
like the steering wheel
and then
to emphasize the ride is over
raises both hands
and lets you go

the screeching screaming warning
of impending separation
takes so very long
to fade away

Crotchety

Have you noticed, he asks,
That woman in the house across
Who talks to her cats
As though they were human?
One day last summer
I heard her reading to them—
poetry for heaven's sake,
And matching the rhythm of the verses
To the twitching of their tails.
Made my hair stand on end
And my spine run goosebumps.

Do you believe, I still recall
Exactly, every line?
Here, let me say it for you,
It was meant to be repeated:

"Come kitty, kitty, kitty
Where art thou hiding now?
Art seeking mice, or scratching lice,
Or cleaning off thy brow?
If thou art under my bed yet,
I swear thee one time more,
There are no man's shoes there to find
Not there, nor by the door.
Come kitty, kitty, pretty please
And I will read thee verses
To free us from our wounded hearts
And broken love's harsh curses.
We are alone, dost thou not know
He'll ne'er to us come home?
Come sip this wine of words with me,
And let the bastard roam."

Does it make you shiver too?
She slammed the book shut,
Closed her eyes, leaned back
And said (I thought to *me*)

"Well, did you like the poem, my dear?
Would you leave *your* shoes lying,
Lying insincerely under a bed of lust,
Let them gather the dust of broken dreams
While you carelessly break your pledges?
What hedges would you skulk behind,
What games of hide and seek
With her poor heart, poor heart.
He's torn mine all apart I fear,
Irreparable damage.

Damn my age and immobility.
I close my eyes and see the gate
Swinging empty as he walked away
That day, that wretched afternoon.
To never love 'til kingdom come
Would be too soon. I rather prefer
Blood in my veins to his rhyming deceit."

She opened her eyes, saw me staring,
Shouted some obscenity
And drew the curtains.

I am turning into a crotchety old woman who talks to her cats and lives life on the page of a poem and I don't want any man's shoes under my bed or words in my heart wreaking havoc again.   (Emily, 1997)

poem of blessing

your words flow in my thoughts
and in my veins, as though
you were my natural sister
not a stranger with a pen
who cuts me rapier wide
with every new description
of overwhelming sorrow
of overpowering joy

you are in my heart, my head
as familiar as the ones
around my supper table
around the hasty coffins
we have both seen filled
weeping for the silent days
empty of their laughter
empty of their love

your pain rolls down my face
until i cannot tell if
these are your tears or mine
your stories or my memories
and i know without pause
that knowing you, reading you
fills me with a gentle hope
for better tomorrows

and so i call a blessing down
as one might call the rain
on fields of drought
a blessing on your head
and on your house

coronary care

bled of oxygen,
thicker than the deepening blue
of the dying sky
he comes to her
empty, exhausted

she pulses with life
replenishes him
his near-dead burgundy
swirled and saturated
until he glows scarlet

but there is no rest
and he is forced away
to share the bounty
with every needy stranger
until again
empty and exhausted
he flows, depleted,
into her waiting chambers

grass was taller

sheep springs
is clearly in the
   middle of nowhere
not four-corners qualified
or capitol of anything
it boasts only the trading post
a small cafe and
the chapter house mandated
by tribal headquarters
for local...

   in reservation terms
   that would mean something
   between 50 and 100 square miles
   of sand and sagebrush
   interspersed with dry washes
   arroyos that can fill
   and kill in an instant
   when rain on distant mountains
   comes too much too fast and
      finding it cannot seep down
      into the earthy womb that opened for
      the first kachinas and the
      afterbirth of navajo mythology
   flees the hills and rushes dirty red
   down the previously mentioned
   dry washes without warning
   across highways
   where dips instead of bridges
   surprise unwary tourists

   ... meetings and events of grave importance
   like the theft of hosteen's saddle
   the one his father gave him
   u.s. cavalry insignia
   still deeply embossed ...

hosteen recounts again
    how the soldier with the sad eyes
    had no other apology
    after the infamous long walk
    simply took the saddle from his horse
    set it at father's feet
    and rode away bareback
    shoulders slumped with the burden
    of turning warriors into shepherds
because the telling of the story
is a vital page in their book of remembering

… which the tribal police duly noted
and will watch for at
the fair at window rock
the rodeo at shiprock
though everyone knows there is little hope
the saddle will be found

while hosteen slowly shakes his head
at the loss of this piece of his past
his face shows no emotion
for that is not the navajo way
instead he talks of days
when the now dry reservation grew green
with grass that reached the stirrups of the
saddle that is gone
the drought that took it all away
days when he could leave things
atop his corral and they would stay
it is not right he says
that the honor of our people
has dried up like that grass

navajo weaver

her loom is handmade
sheep handraised
wool handsheared
handcleaned and handcarded

plants for dyes
she handpicked with her cousin
when the color of the evening sky
behind the starkness of spider-woman rock
hung hazy muted lavender
like russian thistle blossoms
dried and steeped for hours
the water waiting only the yarn
of what would be for her
another labor of need
need to pay a bill
feed a family
grandchildren too young
to be of any help
children gone here and there
some to work
some to drink
one to california

the pattern grows
row by row
mind to hand to thread
  it was a full winter ago
  this thread was spun
  when the snow was too deep
  for even their horse to challenge
  the snows had caught them unprepared
  and except for emergency food
  and hay helicoptered in
  they would have grown very thin

but would not have complained
would not have dared offend
the earth, the gods, the elements
by seeming ungrateful for life
however harsh
she never draws her patterns
simply conceives them
and weaves them into something
she hopes will please the trader
    she pauses thinking ahead
    how they will bargain politely
    (she taught him the art)
    and she will feel she has won
    if she takes home an extra bag of flour
    the twenty-five-pound bluebird brand
    and cash enough for gasoline
doesn't worry past that or wonder
who will own her latest work
and will they understand the *ch'iindi* trail
the purposeful imperfect line
woven in to let her spirit out

today she wonders only
why the child in california
is so silent

i know the where and why

i know the where and why
of every kiss
the sudden loss of innocence
beneath the pressing passion
of lips hard and hungry
or soft and seductive—

times, places, and most of all
their faces are here
etched in polished granite
that reflects the years
scoffs at the vapors
the night mists
the ghostly memories
that come tapping
tapping for attention

i know the where and why
of every kiss
the early lust, the later love
deep and determined
the quick hello, the lingering goodbye
the unexpected rush of passion
rediscovered

i wonder if a winter tree
feels some vague loss
or shivers with regret
for a summer now gone

i stand alone
hands tracing the rocky record
and i smile—
i know the where and why
of every kiss

water line

toad will think nothing
of the constant hand
that keeps the lilies clear
grooming the shading leaves
and quiet water
that all but guarantee
progeny to infinity
in the absence
of plastic
of paper
of tin

heron will ignore him
think nothing of the clearness
of the pool he fishes
bent only on the catch
that glimmers near the shore

simplicity
a long pole rake and canvas bag
brought daily to this pond
erasing the indifference
of fast-food trash
and careless hands
along the water line

lamentation

i am no isaiah
though i too have unclean lips
sins like scarlet
and night dreams
of some glorious future
beyond my reach

ezekiel
saw the valley
where bones parched and dry
arose and put on flesh
i am just a dry bone
thirsty and alone
in this valley of dust

mostly i sit
with jeremiah
and let the tears of my heart
flow against the floor of reality
imperfect man
in an imperfect world
preparing for the worst
hoping for more
than wasting away
prisoner
to all that i am not

some afternoon

he is gone, he is gone
news travels fast, and faster
when it is hard to bear
i feel a forming thunder-cloud
prediction of the flood to come
not so much sorrow for the dead
as for the living left alone
who will turn some afternoon
to share a thought or laugh
before the embarrassed pain
when he is not where we expect him

it took me years past her dying
to stop thinking
i must share this or that
with mother, she will laugh
and ask for repetitions

we miss them every one
those who go but not completely
walking the halls and corners of our minds
quietly waiting those moments
those unexpected afternoons
when we address them with
a sentence, a song, a sudden smile
before reality descends and covers them
in drapes of sad remembering

letting

never mind that science
with its infinite disdain
for things deemed metaphysical
superstitious, mystical
spits on what we do here

my lancet and cannula
boldly breach your waiting vein
i monitor the outflow of humors
dark and therefore poisoned

we are such old friends
you bleed for me willingly
trusting i will know precisely
the second to desist
congratulate your deliverance
from the devils that beset you

blackout

imagine the artist's face
one evening as he left—
his private mona lisa
handing him his brushes
a half-finished canvas
the little hat he loved
all in a bag
as she vanished
through the doorway
turned the lock

i think he would paint poorly
for a long, long time
every color on the palette
would mock him
remind him of some interplay
of light and shadow
the hue of an eye
full of laughter

whether he sketched
the kitchen window
or the parson's children
every picture would be her face
until he stopped painting light at all
moving to browns and blacks
more somber than rembrandt
coming to the day he covered the canvas
entirely black, stood back
and tossed his brushes in the fire

landlocked

two lanes go through my town
faded shoulder stripes
double yellow warning in the middle:
DO NOT CROSS
and here or there the makings
of yet another pothole

yesterday i closed my eyes
trying to remember
the sound of seagulls
the kick of salt spray
heavy odors of a low-tide beach
and nothing came
nothing came

songs unsung

one moment he was there
then he was not
some combination
of someone with too much car
and too much drink
erased him from my pages

maybe we weren't so close
as some friends are
but i had to turn quickly
when i heard
hide the tears
carry on the task
that occupied the moment

that night i sat in bed
not caring if the covers stained
let thought and emotion flow
worried less for me
than for those who gave him voice
knowing they would live the pain
of all his songs unsung

just to paint

her childish eyes sparkled
with stars not yet gone out
smile like a crescent moon
as jar after jar of tempera powder
came down from the cupboard

trembling hands waited for brushes
ready to splash fields of gold
starry nights and boats adrift
on paper that never came

"too small" echoed through her heart
"when you're older" ground against her mind
the damp, dark blanket of being denied
settling over her spark

she never cried, gave no hint at all
of the devastation, the darkness and despair
desire walled away like poe's amontillado
bones instead of beauty

forgotten feelings until today
when a random picture tugged against her heart
pulled loose the keystone
spilled the bricks that hid her fire

a gasp and a self-reveal
the sad eyes of a little girl
who just wanted to paint

whisper the name

too early born, she challenged them
keep me if you can
and i will also fight
to prove love is not wasted

she did not know her father's fear
the uncertainty of her smallness
a spear that pierced his heart, his faith

he hesitated to lean down
could not allow himself enough hope
to breathe the name of God
into her tiny ear

each day came with the question
was it time and should he speak
bless her and make her holy
or would he offend deity
break himself on rocks of grief
if the fragile shell
around her solid spirit
fractured and fell away

every morning until day twenty five—
then with the joyful reassurance
of everyone who had touched her
fed her, held her here
he took her gently up
and lips to ear spoke just two names
Allah's first
then hers

dead poets

yes i know that cummings
also shunned upper case
and elliott wrote
things simply complex
with endings that often stood
alone and apart
severed tails
staring bewildered at the body
of the poems that dropped them
unexpectedly
on dirty london sidewalks

i am torn
between the pleasure of
swimming deep in the poetry
of browning, frost, and sandburg,
keats, and yeats, and donne and more

torn because i know
how easily i imitate
put on someone else's clothes
sing songs in voices that were
never mine, though not completely strange

there is a fear
founded or otherwise
that i will forget myself
fade into a poor reflection
of poets past and passing
lose my own clear voice
in the colors of countries

times and places i never knew
and so i am surprised
when someone says
you write like so and so
and is he or she or they
your true favorite
idol, model, mentor in absentia

when the embarrassment
the redding of ignorance passes
i promise to be better
build on the foundation
left by every predecessor
even read a work or two
of the most recently quoted
but resolve proves sand-like
and i
irresolute
begin another portrait
with the brush-and-oil words at hand
if i will not be burns
or milton or millay
i must be j.

come night

come night!
full of mystery
dark and foreboding
blanketing the harshness
of the bright relentless day
i do not fear you

come night!
cover me with quieting sleep
with soft forgetful dreams
with freedom—
remove the cloth
that binds me to reality
and drop me in
a boundless surreal sea
where time floats
or flies at my command

come night!
swaddle me
in cradles of comfort—
mind and soul and body
will sing or dance or drink
from a fountain of renewing

come night!
when you have run your course
gather gently 'round me
you must not rush away
but fade reluctantly
as though i were a love
you hate to leave

neural fury

across the plasmoid chasm
membrane shrouded forces marshal
swirling in their eagerness
to jump the gap
be swallowed in the mystery
of the other side

unruly, they break across
spinning, leaping, soaring
the fury of a solar flare unleashed
spikes into the opposite wall
unbidden
unwelcome
unhindered
pulsing exuberance
into unsuspecting muscles
i watch, helpless
as giles de tourette
wreaks havoc on my son

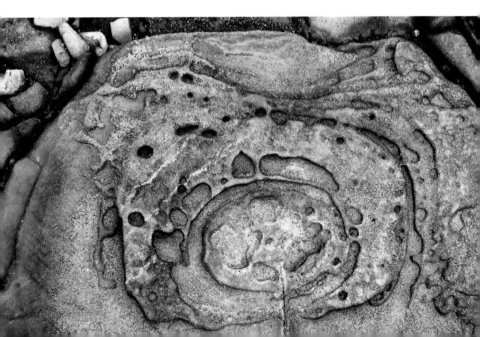

Iron and Ether

Something familiar in the curve,
The anguished bend of steel overcome
By heat and stress beyond belief—
Caught my eye because it was
The essence of you,
Trapped and facing death,
Refusing to yield until
The last possible life
Had slipped to safety.

I bought the photograph.

All I have of you
Are the vapors of memory,
One of three thousand missing
And logically dead.
Still, you are as solid in my mind
As that monument of iron,
Arching as though to shield me
From the emptiness ahead.

can't hide from mama

unless you get too technical
by nineteen i was gone
and whatever mama wanted me to learn
was done, finished, over

college and family and work—
i left new mexico behind
nothing there to pull me back
no tsk-tsk to irritate me
aggravate me when i insisted
on spinning the wheel
and taking whatever number
fell beneath my hand

somewhere along the way mama up and died
and i said goodbye out loud
done at last with her looking over my shoulder
oversized frown at some choice
i felt was mine alone to make

no one warned me 'bout mama's ghost
the one that sneaks
into the middle of a good dream
finger wagging in my face
and i wonder how'd she get there
and how much did she see—

on a cloudy day, sometimes
she slips into a stream of thought
leaving me to wonder
if maybe i wasn't son enough

and then there's times
like just this afternoon
when the lady in the next car
window down, yapping like a chihuahua
wants to school me in the fine art of driving
(and i already knew she never graduated that one)
and the impulse flashes, and my hand starts to raise
and the single-digit salute is already forming
but i can't, just can't
'cause i feel mama watching

backyard

the bricks along the flower bed
still want straightening
a daily reminder
they should have been set deeper
or in cement

the grass pretends
that bare spots are beauty marks
and goes about being greenest
under a flowering crabapple tree

the hollyhocks, once confined
have jumped the bricks
and stubbornly refuse to be restrained

sweet peas wave their frail pastels
in a shy hooray, hurrah
just enough of them
to bouquet our sunday table

chrysanthemums have been replaced
by yellow crookneck squash
more plant than produce
spreading leaves large and proud
against the dull gray cinderblocks
that keep them from our neighbor

the backyard of my childhood
slips into my mind in quiet times
when i need the innocent laughter
of running barefoot 'round the tree
while mother hung out clothes

children

are these not the small eyes
that unjudging accepted my imperfect face
translated the likeness
into a full smile no wider
than the length of my littlest finger

are these not the tiny hands
that held my heart
with their clumsy instinctive grasp
and later with innocent trust
as we walked together
kicking first autumn leaves
into the frosty air

what am i to do with them
these eyes wide with wonder
that see too well
my more imperfect face
these hands that trace
a heart grown harder
against the winds of life

they see me and know me as i am
and lips that once amused me
with childish babblings
affirm their parentage
and still are not ashamed

last ride

joseph always knew
the end would come
it comes for everyone

he could not have known
that he would come to this
robbed of speech
thought
movement
body winding down

i see his spirit
tall and joyful
standing on the station platform
white-haired halo shining
one hand holds
his hallelujah bag
one is raised in hope
as the last train slows

joseph takes
a longing look
at those who stay behind
then he is gone

gemstone

you are hard she said
hard-headed
hard-hearted
hard-won

wedge and mallet struck
and something more
of the rough
brittle exterior
fell away
a tiny sparkling facet
rewarded the blow

you are hard she said
hard-driving
hard-hitting
hard-handed

another plane of cleavage
yielded to her relentless pressure
again the prism flashed

you see yourself
as common stone
but you will be
the center jewel
in my crown

she held me to the light
smiled
and lifted the mallet again

semper fido

low throaty growl
slow twitching tail
and the quiver of an almost snarl
mark the plot of a dogged dream
as if dogs did such things

dream i mean
wondering why people insist
on humanizing pets
heck
why not say
instead of treeing cats
the half-bared fang
is an unconscious reaction
to my having read him
my latest poem tonight
the one in seven syllables
when anyone who knows dogs
could tell you they prefer
free verse
and short lines

poor furry friend
tomorrow he will sit on the porch
gnawing his rawhide bone
counting on his toes to see
if i missed a beat somewhere
begging me with big sad eyes
never to read him again
a piece with such rigid meter

hush for the sax

hush.
listen to the melody
the undulating voice of pain
too wide for hands to hold
too deep for hell's own shadows
too mute to resist

hush.
feel the empty agony
of unexpected loneliness
the heart-torn tone of tears
that only a musician could cry
and only a woman bear, unmoved

hush.
sense the final, lowest note
descending beneath the human ear
to resonate eerily through the floor
of this darkened convocation

hush.
bathe in the flow
of this blues bar
orphean saxophone

leaves

one evening it was summer
shirtsleeves and football
dragging on past supper
then chores and letters
finally bed

next morning i awoke
to the sounds of autumn
rattling yellow and brown
against my window
there were breath-clouds
as i gathered the daily news
from the porch already half covered
in the falling splendor
of shade trees going to sleep

it wasn't long after
that winter washed away
this year's memories
replacing them with focus
on the here and now of staying warm
huddled by a heat vent
or piling on three sweaters
in a futile rebellion against the cold
the persistent penetrating freeze
much like the feeling
of friendship suddenly gone

my heart would have frozen too
except that i remembered
the greening of my world
when reluctant patches of snow
yielded silently to spring
buds on trees promising more

marking the perennial cycle
of emptiness filled
and the dead brown loneliness
painted over gently
with the colors of an old friend's eyes
come home again

cowboys don't cry

cowboys don't cry his father said
and lessons learned early stayed late
forcing a false machismo on him
he camouflaged his tears
to run with the big boys

tonight the cowboy died
sitting on his sofa
tv news a grim portrayal
of death, destruction, and pain—
the faces of the children
already as still
as the graves they would fill

he wasn't ready
had no time to close doors
draw curtains, throw up walls
and so the cowboy died
washed out by a flood of tears
he could not stop

the eyes of an unbelieving father
child dead in his helpless arms
haunted him for days until he knew
why cowboys never have children

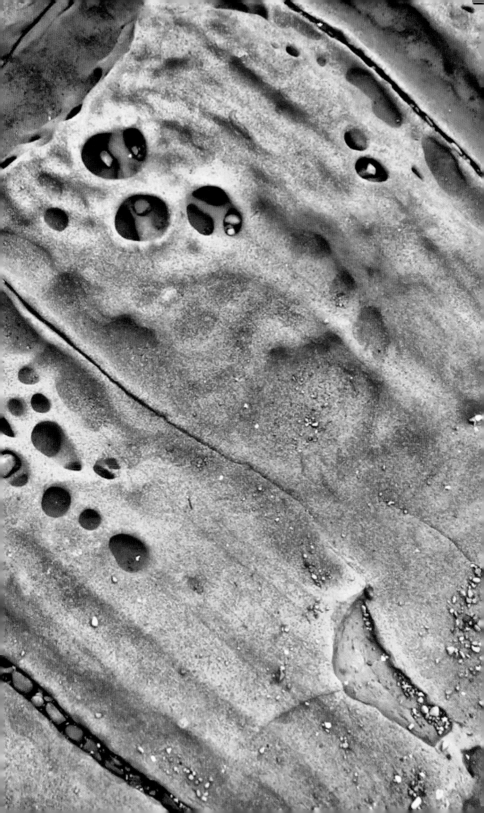

six-eight time

slow and bluesy
i listen to the piano
lay the foundation
for the hungry voice
that whispers and wails
how she feels like a natural woman
and somehow it's my fault

i ignore her boastful lament
concentrate on the chords
tonic
dominant seventh
walk the bass down
modulate
i think i have it
and the keys under my fingers
reluctantly agree

singers are never in short supply
and one who has loitered
outside the door of my practice room
is happy to provide the voice
in fact already knows the words
the emphasis and pauses
that make this piece thrill me
i shiver as she ends soft and low

the conversation after
leads somehow to dance
she claims the meter of a song
can just pick you up
and slam-dunk drop you in love
with whomever you're with at the time
wants to demonstrate

so the needle meets the vinyl
sets the bluesy piano off again
she slips her arms around me
begins to move in six-eight time
and there i am in love
forever
or at least
until the song ends
and i don't even know her name

soft hearted

i had forgotten until today
the summer that we kept pigs
one boar, one sow
and later, piglets

i think the plan was
they were coming to dinner
when they had reached
some arbitrary scale
and were judged sufficient to join us

i was small then
water buckets like lead weights
splashing with every step
as i struggled from the faucet to the sty
slop buckets reeked
of stale fried eggs
and coffee grounds
of gravy and grease

i despised the pigs
for their eager expectation
as though this garbage
were a waldorf meal
despised them too
because they weren't my idea
(i was fine with packaged bacon)
but father said
he wasn't raising pigs
he was raising boys to men
a philosophy that struck me then
as being something like
the ankle deep manured mud
that kept the porkers happy

my father was a farm boy
reality for him was harsh
life was not asked to be fair
and when one defective piglet
proved he could die
more easily than he could live
there was no burial
we left him in the sucking mire
surrounded by a family
unaware of his passing

i learned later
they had him for dessert
after the buckets and i were gone
but since big boys don't cry
i grieved for him silently
and wondered who would miss me
if i also proved defective

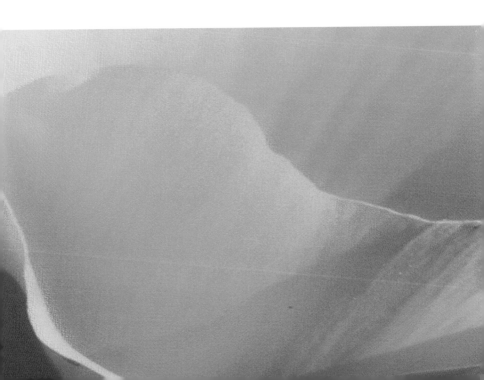

jail shoes

he could have been a grown-up oliver
though not so innocent
still naively pleading
please sir

his chart note stated casually
recently condemned to one hundred plus years
he may need mental health to check on him

he asked again for dispensation
not for pity or forgiveness
focused only on the heel, the right heel
the one that had been broken
thinking
damn i can't do a hundred years
in plastic sandals
i can't even do a week
and jail staff tell me
only medical approves special shoes

i wavered briefly
distracted by frigid, rigid rules
that spell out who
and why and when

i didn't know and quickly realized
i didn't care why
a hundred years
saw only a man in pain
and through him, family
torn by this recent reality
trying to comprehend
a sentence longer than life
asking only for the smallest mercy
something i knew was absolutely in my power
to grant or deny to someone not so innocent

he repeated his naive request
please sir
may i have my shoes

quietly

outside the circle
of family and friends:
silence.
no celebration over new life
she came quietly
grew as some girls do
into a woman
full of purpose and promise
sparkle and hope of motherhood
in her dark eyes
she never bore a child
chose instead to walk
among the children of sorrow
hunger and death
pulling them close
arms of iron faith
gentle around them

she had nothing, wanted nothing
except the means to hold at bay
the sharp teeth of poverty
misery and loneliness
for the small ones
who learned to call her "mother"

years past the fading of any worldly beauty
she carried within a greater light—
small hands that touched her face
innocently assumed that angels all have wrinkles

we knew her name, her deeds, her heart
though few followed the lamp she lifted
she was a gift to those who would have
no other gift in life

and when the last drops of her compassion
had gone to quench some grateful thirst
she left as she had come
quietly

the sun is rising

the sun is rising in Nigeria
scattering sleep like leaves
running for their lives from the
growl of a gas powered chainsaw
that throws dreams loosely side to side
until they fall into the streets
to be crushed by every passing car
or truck or bicycle intent on getting
somewhere more important than where
it is at the moment

the sun is rising in Nigeria
calm yellow light that paints hope
over the soiled walls of war
pushes shadowy fears deep into
alleys and corners to be questioned
later when we have awakened fully
when the dullness of too much death
and too little sleep is eased aside
by conversations with friends
by the discovery of an unexpected poem
scribbled on the pull-down doors
of a random shop that hasn't yet
opened to smile us in for coffee

the sun is rising in Nigeria
lifted from its own ragged sleep
by the songs of children who
know nothing of peace and
everything of instant happiness
in the giggling games they play—
lifted by the rhythmic rhymes
of poets who know better but
cannot stop believing that this day
newly birthed will somehow be
the day when no one dies

first lie

the knot in my stomach
grew tighter and tighter
deceitful thought
became word
averting punishment
and suddenly
i knew
like adam in the garden
cain in the field
truth could be hidden
under fig leaves
or shallow dirt—
i laughed
it was so easy

then the whispers came
again and again
calling to me
asking for explanations
for abel
until i had
no answer
but the truth

full of the cold

i am full of the cold
internally snow, infernally slow
ice in my veins and a frozen heart
casually sculpted by her unkind hands
into a caricature of caring

i am full of the cold
numb past recovering
dumbfounded at the ease of the freeze
the offhanded way she took a little
here and there until my icy stare
suited her fancy for crystals

i am full of the cold
head to toe quiescence
the very essence of winter
no hint of spring
no sign of anything higher than zero
entropy fading, leaving no heat
no hope

no more

summer sings in me no more, no more
the gladness of the new dawn as a dream
faint and nearly vanished like a mist
in heat of sun that knows not to implore
a kindness from the vaporizing beam
dissipates and leaves me only this—
a half-remembered smile, a touch, a kiss
and silence where her laughter rang before

just me and the music

stretching into the night
mottled black and gray
punctuated by the nonsense code
of dashes and dots
the freeway hums against the beat
of the radio

my free foot
the one not on the gas
keeps time
while i, unabashed
force the high harmony
to fill the pickup cab
no one there to care
if i miss a word or two
break to falsetto
when the notes move too high
or cough
when the bass beckons me
and i, silly tenor
try to slide down
somewhere i only go
when i have a cold—

but i don't have to think
don't have to miss you
don't have to worry
about tomorrow's early alarm
or taxes or children or anything
no—
tonight
on this empty four-lane
there is only me
and the music

one year after

a month has passed
a few weeks maybe
or an eternity ago
since the day you called

it was your sister's birthday
the negative news not overly bad
so we didn't set in worrying
not like we would
too soon

that was the early warning
and we prayed with you
that the cyclone of possibilities
would pass by to the east or the west
just not over you, not over us

but the sirens that screamed
hide your heart in the cellar
got louder, more shrill until
that calm quiet eye
the hold-your-breath center
hovered over you
confirming that this would be
your worst storm ever

you stepped into the whirlwind again
preparations for the inevitable
what to do and when
who to tell and what
how to keep a grip on your heart
on your sanity

then pain, enough to rip you open
and love, enough to hold you together
until nightfall when the weather's fury faded
leaving devastation, disbelief, and sorrow
too deep to plumb

we cried with you
we cried for you and for us all
because there was nothing more to do
the tiny spark of life
that tried so hard to flicker in
slipped out silently
and that was that

so reconstruction started
new foundations, walls, and ceilings
built over and around your ache
took months to pull together
we pulled for you as though
we could saint-like hold darkness back
until you found your light
we cried at every new writing
of your grief, your longing, your emptiness
and we waited

one year after
the memory of Christian promised
the emptiness of Christian gone
is building thunderclouds
threatening new storms
asking ominously
will the fragile walls
come down

dopamine

he is not in the details
as i was often told
not smoking fiery red
no horns
no fork
no tail

no
the devil is in the dopamine
sliding into synapses
overriding receptors
interfering with the best intentions
afferent and efferent impulses
blocked
diverted
enhanced
as love and lust
motivation and addiction
adoration and adultery
swirl in sensual spirals
tiptoe through thoughts
dance across dreams

i am puppet to the stream
of chemicals flowing
never knowing
who controls the rails
on the mesolimbic line
is the engineer today
infernal or divine

ocean crossing

come sail away she calls to me
leave behind the solid shore
abandon aging fears
self-whispered lies of
always being less
why drown in seas of doubt

follow wind and current
i will show you
seven seas of wonder

leave behind the shadows
of cliff and cave alike
dance on my moonlit decks
to the rhythm of wave
to the siren call
of endless ocean
boundless dreams
come sail away with me

secrets

where do you turn when you are young
and the guilt of sins real or imagined
daily grinds and nightly devours you?

older years would know
to seek a father confessor
or a friend's ear,
might choose to drown the voices
with the contents of one bottle or another

i remember those days
gray and hopeless
when heaven was too far
and no one knew
and no one cared
that the small boy
with the worried face
was dying from his secrets
not knowing how to live
not daring to stop living

that hell is gone
but the memories stay

at odd moments a child's face
or a parent oblivious
pulls them up and plays them
fresh and crisp as memorex

i hold my own child in my arms
sad little worried face
afraid to promise he will find in me
what i could never find
when i was young

response to rain

news footage and online video
carefully avoided to skip the tears
i only see him in my mind
where she painted his struggling plea
knees in the red sand, bleeding
for every friend and countryman
pulled down, laid down too soon

i see the rain clouds forming
sense sentinel drops, then deluge
as nature bends to help him purge
the unnatural evil that claws
at everything, everyone he knows

i see his upturned face
wet with the thundering gift
grief and faith and gratitude
mixed in his tears, in the rain
and i cry with him, for him
for a county i don't know
for brothers and sisters unmet
for the violence in my own streets
ceaseless, senseless death
wondering if there will ever be
rain enough to cleanse us all

roundness of dragon

let go your notions of wings
of long snaky bodies
scales and talons too--
let them go up in dragon flame
come to me
come

i am a roundness of dragon
head like an aging friar's
sun-touched and gleaming
over sumo-bellied beauty
and legs to make Rubens weep for joy
come to me
come

i will of course devour you
your stories, poems, tears
hopes, dreams
and lust (yes, i know how that burns)
every bit of you chewed slowly
the bones of your personality
picked clean by questioning
until the skeleton of your history
stands naked in my gaze

when i am satisfied
that you hold nothing more
to feed my endless curiosity
fatten my treasure-hoard of knowing
then i will whisper
go from me
go

piano man

left hand rolls
rockin' boogie bass
right hand frolics
with a melody
feet tapping
like st. vitus on fire

song's end
both hands glide
down the entire tusk
and without pause
pick up a slow
through your heart
and out your mind
blues rhythm

i see him
smile at the sax
who slips in mellow
full of pain

goose bumps
i get goose bumps
for these blues
my fingers drumming softly
the table where
your hand rested
yesterday

difference

the difference he said
is not so obscure
or even hard to describe—
they care and we don't

you insult me, i write you off
or ignore you and get on with the game
because the game after all is paramount
and winning is still everything

tomorrow
i will have forgotten because we won
and winning means forgetting grudges
forgiving offenses and celebrating
or because we lost and losing means
planning for the next battle

not so the other sex
an unkind cut is taken to heart
and even the smallest wounds
bleed long beyond a victory or defeat
everything is personal and poignant
and therefore perpetual

the difference really is he said
that they care and we don't

prelude to hopelessness

war at home or just over the border
and coming for you soon enough
calamities calling
howling your name in the whirlwind
growling your name in the rumbling shift
of continental plates
nature uneasy, no respite

sleep rolls in restless dreams
waking to stress on stress
politics pound contradictions
waste and pollution cling
to everything they touch until
resolve is overcome
dissolves
and leaves you staring dully
at a starless future

supper table

for arthur henry king

arthur was my father
though not first
nor even yet the second
those honored places given
first to God
then earthly sire
i loved him not less

arthur was my hero
holding easily at hand
a knowledge of language
places and people
so broad i could not ford
so deep i found no footing
so humble i believed
i could be like him

arthur sat at table
where we had come together
after years apart
and though i knew his ailment
i knew nothing
until i saw the tremors
and the clouded glance
where steadiness and a keen eye
had kept court in kinder years—

his mortality
his frailty
a harsh confrontation
i was ill-prepared to face—
a haunting picture
that troubles me
when i try not to remember

arthur will inevitably pass
some morning, noon or night
while i am off pursuing
the excellence he taught me
could be mine—
and i will wait for someday
when arthur sits at table
wrapped not in failing flesh
but clothed in glory

siren call

they are here in my head
lingering, haunting melodies
the musical clink of gold coins
promises of life unburdened

i follow them through the litany
of simple steps to separation
from here, from now
but never from her

the move would glide so smoothly
pack the clothes and computers
load the truck and go
find a new place somehow
somewhere
make new friends
and bank the bonus
at little cost to me

but she is deaf, hears no music
feels no pull, no longing
only fear multiplied
every time i think aloud
she sees the price in tears
in loss, in loneliness

her ears are filled with beeswax
so tie me to the mast
and keep the charted course

face value

i do not ever want
to be taken at face value
this face is of no worth
nothing hollywood about it
no symmetry, no serenity
and precious little character

no, i want to be taken
at faceless value
taken for what quiet deeds
and anonymous gifts i can give
like the surprise in an inmate's eyes
when his anger is met with
quiet respect and kindness

when the final accounting is done
my deepest hope will be
that Heaven looks past my worthless face
and deep into my heart to find
the price of passage home

Le Gigot Qui Pleure*

Recipe/Rosary

Take a leg of lamb
  Oh, Lamb of God, the lone, the great I AM
Spike with slivered garlic cloves
  Whose wounded side was cruelly pierced for me
Rub with rosemary, salt and pepper
  Then wrapped with fragrant spice
  against the grave—
Place in preheated oven for one hour, collect drippings.
  That night thou suffered in Gethsemane
  That wicked men should thus be thine to save,
  Unholy pain caused Holy tears to flow,
Cut potatoes into thin, even slices
  And this thou didst to cut away my sin.
Dot with butter, season with garlic and salt
  O, Balm of Gilead, Savior of all men,
Sprinkle potatoes with fat from roasting lamb
  Thy blood, applied, will cover my transgression.
Put potatoes in oven with lamb and bake until done
  So purify me, Lord, in that same fire
  That I may bend my will to thy desire,
Makes six to eight servings.
  And fit me for thy service, through confession,
  That I may sup with thee, thou Weeping Lamb.

"Weeping Leg of Lamb"— French Recipe

contrails

be scientific, be intellectual
lecture me on cirrus aviaticus
how hot exhaust and particulates
condense and dance and disperse
over seconds, minutes, days, weeks—
tickle my brain with explanations
of contrail climate change

be magical, be mysterious
whisper to me how the ghosts
of every airline disaster
float behind those jets
billowy white fingers reaching
stretching for miles
clawing their way aboard

be ignorant, be earthbound
explain to me how you never once
look up to see those water lines
raking fingernails across a chalkboard sky
never bother with things so far away
when each spring's preoccupation
is that the creek will rise too high
flooding out the garden sprouts
each summer is spent fretting
that it will run too low
and all the corn will wither

be lyrical, be poetic
write lines that catch my breath
before i exhale into winter air
my own vapor trail that marks
if only for an instant
my passage through your life

the weight of things

carnitas super burrito
has a beautiful rhythm to it
when said with the "r"
and rolled "double r"
which i have carefully learned
to imitate so as to not be
misunderstood when ordering

i wonder if they ever put one
of these gastronomical monsters
on a scale to see just how far
it would tip before going over

my wager, having hefted one,
is for a pound and a half plus a little
thankfully, the bulging tortilla
does not venture a guess
about my gravitational pull

i pay for the foil-wrapped feast
which is carefully placed
in a plain brown bag "para llevar"
and handed to me, hot

so hot in fact that I quickly
shift my grip to just the corner
of the bag, and begin a slow fight
with gravity's interest in my meal

but i am quick and clever
and soon the beast and i
are at table together where
it doesn't take long to admit
that the burro is stronger than
my appetite and will only tolerate
being half-eaten tonight

not an hour later, the stomach
wakes up crying "feed me, feed me"
but i know exactly where the scale
and i stop being friends, so
i am eating grapes and chanting
"half a burrito is more than enough"

tonight, there will be guacamole dreams

can we just reincarnate

wouldn't it be great she asked
if we could just reincarnate
drop these tired, broken bodies
and step into new flesh, new bones
new sneakers and new jeans

she laughed at the thought
pulled a photo from a red clutch
as tired and worn as she was
look: me at sixteen
full of ambition and no direction
sixty was nowhere in my mind
my heart, my bones
like it is today

do you think age has weight
she wondered aloud
and answered herself
i do, yes i do
everything feels heavier
harder to hold up
harder to hold onto

she thinks about her uncle
and his heaviness
of heart, of mind, of body
tries to fathom his loneliness
that universal unique pain
of separation, of sorrow
the turning to one no longer there
to complain or whisper his love

just today someone said
at least she this or that
at least he something else
and it was meaningless
wasted words
and no comfort at all

she looks up suddenly and smiles
remembering she is not alone
though she has been more often than not
more often when it mattered most
do you know how hard it is
starting over again at sixty
with new work, new wrinkles, new worries

he smiled at the rhetorical question
as he scribbled a new poem
on her napkin
yes, he said quietly, yes

drought

we dance through the heat of noon
dance for rain that never comes
dust drips from faces
burned brown by merciless sun
drips and forms dust pools
under our shuffling feet

we dream of water
of diluvial deliverance
and wake unable to speak
through parched throats
crusted tongues
dull teeth

we cry for our crops
one tear or two over each
faltering, failing plant
the last moisture in us
and then we wait and watch
to see if God will cry with us
break the seal of the sky
and bless us, water us
until harvest

tenses

past perfect:
push a button
roll the film
i had washboard abs
hair enough to get
vidal's attention
the greeks called me adonis

present tense:
how can so few children
seem like so many
why does my job
want to be my life
there's no clean shirt
and today's sandwich
looks like yesterday
i'm late
and there's only oatmeal
for breakfast

future conditional:
if social security doesn't fail
if i still have a head
even with no hair
and no one steals my pension
and the house outlasts us
if the children leave home
if they come back to visit
not to stay...

future perfect:
if you are with me
at the end
i will have won

politico

past gritty streets
where grimy lamps
scratch darkness back
but never enough

the laughter of money
floats like a fog
around the latest excuse
for all who can pay
to congregate,
congratulate each other

through the sparkled crowd
he strums a bold flamenco—
voice like staccato heels
demanding attention
or slow, seductive slides
changing his rhythm to match
the partner in his arms

he pulls this crowd close
a hundred minds as one
in their lust to be noticed
touched with a word, a phrase
a promise that tomorrow
bits of his transferred brilliance
will shine like sequins carefully dropped
marking them as chosen

pizza boy

watch this girl
her intense hunger
sharpened by anticipation
she licks her lips twice
pulling the first huge slice
off the pan too soon
burning her fingers before
she remembers a napkin
and then with the eagerness
of someone who has already forgotten
wraps the strings of stretched cheese
around the perfect point of the triangle
and bites in

her rapid breathing and muffled cries
will tell you it was too hot to handle
but she never learns
and her tongue pays the price
of impatience, of wanting too much
too soon, too fast

but pizza boy is ready
with the cold drinks and ice
calms her, quiets her, laughing
he knows he can wait
until the heat subsides
then savor every mouthful
mozzarella and marinara
peppers and pepperoni
cheese and chewy crust
after all, this anxious girl
only orders supreme

old friend

yesterdays were rich and full
hours of quiet talk
spent savoring our favorite meals
never the common mill-run fare
no, we wrapped friendship
in the aromas of aged asiago
on poached egg
traded opinions
like bites of garlic toast
or soft-ripe avocado
an occasional exotic
like venison sausage
to pique us
test us
tease us into laughter

today in the open market
the softly pungent odor
of hard cheeses and fresh garlic
peeled away the layered years
brought me back to our table
to your tears and mine
to that day of famine
when the last bite was gone
and friendship died hungry

introspection

miles davis
permeates this small room
with music i never thought to like
until i had enough age
spilling over my belt
to understand what soul really is
and here i am examining mine
objectively of course
in the cold and distant way
that only the real occupant can

for those who subscribe to the stars
i am libra though i feel
more like an ancient persian king
weighed in the balance
and found wanting
always wanting

by the numbers i should be fine
count my name and see
five and four and five more
that makes magic twelve
and two left over for luck

but i believe in neither stars nor numbers
and in this small room
filled with the muted jazz
that only miles can play like himself
i toy with the ghosts of my past
puzzled at the depths of error
and the heights of joy
that drift past for review
what a strange thing i have been for me
stranger still for you

across the open sea

sailing is not my profession
but i understand the metaphors
the talk of wind and waves
of safe harbors and clear skies
trusting the captain who
has prepared and knows
every port along the way

but i am so long robbed
of the sight of land
of blossomed trees and
golden sand between my toes
that i cannot rest until
i see the captain's charts
know at the very least
how far until next port
and something under my feet
not in constant motion

what good-hearted captain
would leave me swabbing a deck
deny me a glimpse at the maps
when one look in my eyes
one look into my soul
would tell him how close
how very close i have come
to losing hope on this
tumultuous open sea

distance doesn't matter much

a voice subtly flavored with a culture
that an ocean holds away from me
calls me by my african name
a name i love but did not earn
and asks me to listen to hearts
to the rhythm of lives daily
torn by bombs and bullets
executions and kidnappings
interlaced with childish songs
children playing in the streets
as they do everywhere, every day

a voice i have never heard aloud
speaks to me urgently asking
if i have seen, if i have felt
the tremors that shake the streets
that make his arteries rattle
his veins tighten and his breath
come in short gasps with every
new story, every news story
until he feels he will never
be able to scream loudly enough
to drown out the images

he asks again if i can hear
his breaking heart

oh, brother, if you knew
the wounds you have carved
with the knife of your words

the holes you have made
in my safe small world with
the bullets of your verses
the stains you have left on
my too-white skin—stains
of the blood of innocents
stains of the angry evil
mobs, armies, gangs, devils
who would force their will
on you, on father, on mother
on child without regard
without regret

yes, i have heard your lament
across an open sea of violence
across a continent of differences
across language and unshared experience
across the pages of what you know
and know how to tell in detail
so minute that to read you
is to feel your smoking pain
your burning passion for
country, family, home
the dark mists of your loss
and under it all
your quiet, unrelenting hope
that you can make life better

yes, brother
i hear your anguished
beautiful voice ring out
across a field of echoes
that distance cannot silence

clear day

ignorant of stars and charts
i slipped into this world naked and helpless
little mr. libra bringing a smile into the pain

growing years ground on me
and though i often failed to please myself
it seemed nothing to be the balance
to another's pain or sorrow
painting peace on today
hope on the face of tomorrow

i always knew that i would be a healer
though the way and the means were cloudy
wandering almost to medicine
then to the compassionate art
man in woman's world
butting against stereotypes
that were too slow dissolving
nursing my own way
providing a corner of calm
in an ocean of sickness and despair

words have been my friends from first babbling
an occasional bit of verse tumbling out on paper
but nineteen ninety six for reasons i may never know
a dam broke and my life came spilling out
poems great and small
detailing pity and passions
that run like a common thread
through everyone i know

we laugh and cry together as they read me
sensing, though not always aloud
the healing of those moments

i never felt i needed describing
but in the middle of her latest wounding
she painted me in one short line
better than i ever drew myself—
you, she said
are a clear day in october

"surgical mass" was first published in *Spark, a Creative Anthology*, Volume I (Empire & Great Jones Little Press)

"avalanche" was first published in *Disorder* (Red Dashboard, LLC)

"empty" was first published as "empty room" in *Disorder* (Red Dashboard, LLC)

"grass was taller" was first published in *The Other Side of Sleep* (Arachne Press)

"andrew in the evening" was first published online by *Painters and Poets Blog*
http://www.paintersandpoets.com

"dopamine" was first published online by *Pigeonholes*
http://pidgeonholes.com

"cardioversion" was first published online by *Right Hand Pointing*
http://www.righthandpointing.net

"Iron and Ether" was first published online by *Synchronized Chaos*
http://synchchaos.com

"old friend" was first published online by *Work to a Calm*
http://worktoacalm.wordpress.com

"introspection" was first published online as "introspectre" by *Work to a Calm*
http://worktoacalm.wordpress.com

"navajo weaver" was first published online by *Foliate Oak Literary Magazine*
http://foliateoak.com

"under the bridge" was first published online by *Oddball Magazine*
http://oddballmagazine.com

"All I Want" was first published online by *One Sentence Poems*
http://www.onesentencepoems.com/osp

"red bridge" was first published online by *Sonic Boom Journal*
http://sonicboomjournal.wix.com/sonicboom

"full of the cold" was first published online by *Cryopoetry*
http://www.cryopoetry.com

"response to rain" and "poem of blessing" were first published online by *Creative Thresholds* — http://www.creativethresholds.com

"across the open sea" was first published online by *The Gnarled Oak*
http://www.gnarledoak.org

"the weight of things" was first published online by *Zetetic: A Record of Unusual Inquiry*
https://zeteticrecord.org

"piano man", "six-eight time", "semper fido", "whisper the name", "backyard", and "jail shoes" were first published online by *Verse-Virtual*
http://www.verse-virtual.com

"hush for the sax" was first published online as "turn down the fires of hell" by *Verse-Virtual* — *http://www.verse-virtual.com*

"lake fog" and "roundness of dragon" were first published online by *Dead Snakes*
http://www.deadsnakes.blogspot.in

"contrails" was first published by *The Hopper*
http://www.hoppermag.org

"politico" was first published online by *Every Day Poems*
http://www.everywritersresource.com/poemeveryday

"dead poets" was first published online by *Literary Yard*
https://literaryyard.com